D0116946

Discovering Dinosaurs

Diplodocus

Aaron Carr

www.av2books.com

AV² provides enriched content that supplements and complements this book. Weigl's AV² books strive to create inspired learning and engage young minds in a total learning experience.

Your AV² Media Enhanced books come alive with...

Go to **www.av2books.com**, and enter this book's unique code.

BOOK CODE

K460964

AV² by Weigl brings you media enhanced books that support active learning.

Audio
Listen to sections of the book read aloud.

Video
Watch informative video clips.

Try This!
Complete activities and hands-on experiments.

Key Words
Study vocabulary, and complete a matching word activity.

Quizzes
Test your knowledge.

Slide Show
View images and captions, and prepare a presentation.

... and much, much more!

Published by AV² by Weigl
350 5th Avenue, 59th Floor
New York, NY 10118

Websites: www.av2books.com   www.weigl.com

Library of Congress Control Number: 2013953028
ISBN 978-1-4896-0584-9 (hardcover)
ISBN 978-1-4896-0585-6 (softcover)
ISBN 978-1-4896-0586-3 (single-user eBook)
ISBN 978-1-4896-0587-0 (multi-user eBook)

Printed in the United States of America in North Mankato, Minnesota
1 2 3 4 5 6 7 8 9 0 17 16 15 14 13

122013
WEP301113

Project Coordinator: Aaron Carr
Art Director: Terry Paulhus

All illustrations by Jon Hughes, pixel-shack.com.

Diplodocus

In this book,
you will learn

what its name means

what it looked like

where it lived

what it ate

and much more!

Meet the Diplodocus.
Her name means "double beam."

4

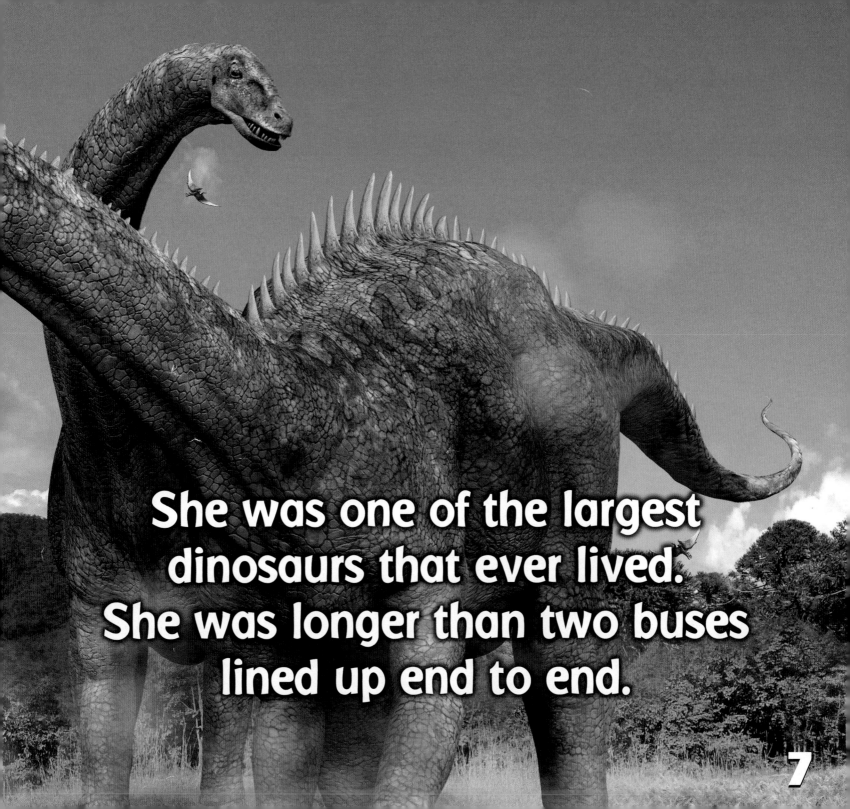

She was one of the largest
dinosaurs that ever lived.
She was longer than two buses
lined up end to end.

She used her long tail
to scare away other dinosaurs.
She could whip her tail
at about 800 miles an hour.
This was fast enough
to make a loud boom.

She was a plant-eater.
She ate many tons of food
every day.

11

She had a very long neck.
She used her long neck
to reach food near the ground
or high up in trees.

She walked slowly
on her four strong legs.

Her top speed was about
15 miles an hour.

She lived in grasslands
near forests and rivers.

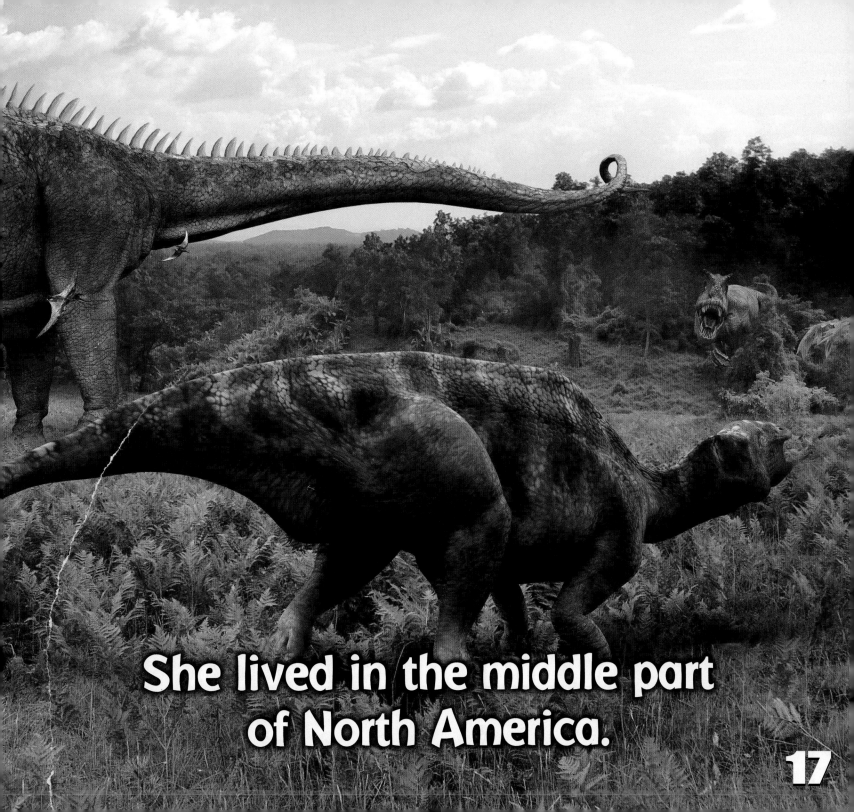

She lived in the middle part
of North America.

She lived about
150 million years ago.

People learned about her from fossils.

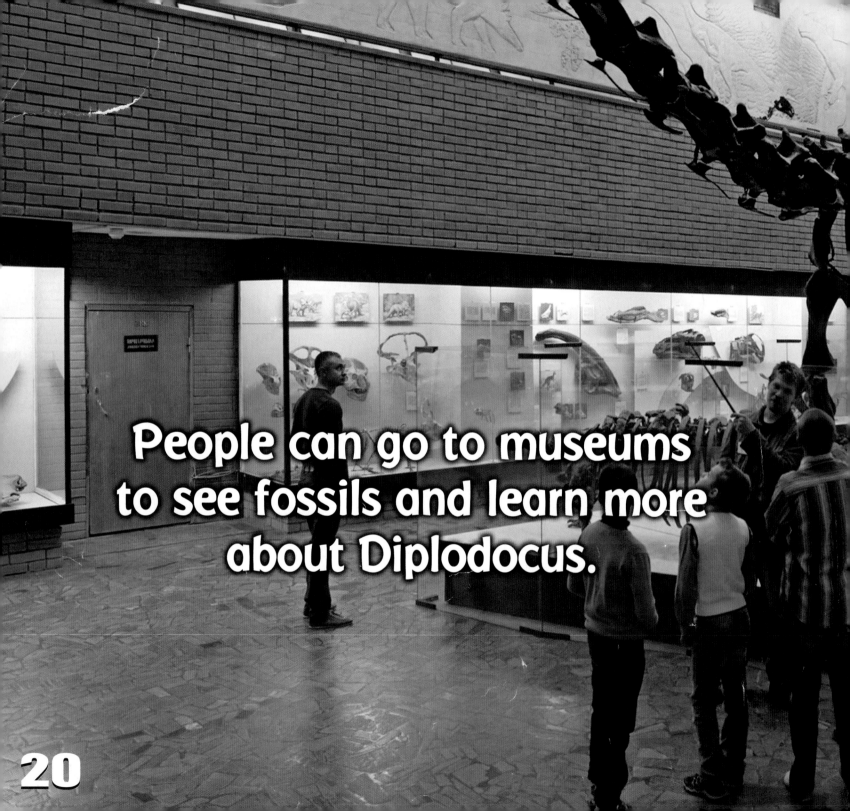

People can go to museums to see fossils and learn more about Diplodocus.

Diplodocus Facts

These pages provide detailed information that expands on the interesting facts found in the book. They are intended to be used by adults as a learning support to help young readers round out their knowledge of each amazing dinosaur or pterosaur featured in the *Discovering Dinosaurs* series.

Pages 4–5

Diplodocus means "double beam." This name comes from two extra bones that ran underneath Diplodocus's spine. This dinosaur also had a distinctive row of spikes running down its neck and back. Diplodocus was part of the sauropod group of massive four-legged dinosaurs. It was related to another large dinosaur called Apatosaurus.

Pages 6–7

Diplodocus was one of the largest dinosaurs that ever lived. Its long tail and neck made Diplodocus one of the longest animals to ever walk the Earth. It was more than 80 feet (24 meters) long, from head to tail. Despite its extreme length, however, Diplodocus was fairly light-weight for its size. Scientists estimate that Diplodocus only weighed about 13 tons (12 metric tons). Similarly sized Apatosaurus weighed nearly 40 tons (35 metric tons).

Pages 8–9

Diplodocus used its long tail to protect itself from predators. Its tail made up about half of its total body length. The tail was flexible, which allowed Diplodocus to use its tail as whip. Recent computer model studies suggest that Diplodocus could whip its tail at speeds close to 800 miles (1,288 kilometers) per hour. This is fast enough to create a very loud sound called a sonic boom. This booming sound could have been used to scare away predators.

Pages 10–11

Diplodocus was a herbivore, or plant-eater. It had to eat tons (metric tons) of food every day in order to support its massive size. Diplodocus likely had a diet made up of conifers, seed ferns, cycads, club mosses, and horsetails. It had about 40 pencil-shaped teeth that it used to strip leaves from branches. Since these teeth were not the right shape for grinding up food, Diplodocus likely swallowed its food whole. It may also have swallowed rocks, which would have helped grind up the food in its stomach.

Diplodocus used its long neck to reach food. Diplodocus had several adaptations that helped it gather such enormous amounts of food. Its long neck allowed Diplodocus to reach into heavily treed areas that its body was too big to fit into. Diplodocus may have also been able to rear up on its hind legs by using its double beam reinforced tail for support. This would have helped Diplodocus reach leaves high up in trees.

Diplodocus walked very slowly on four legs. It had strong, pillar-like legs with five toes on each foot. This made its legs similar to those of an elephant. It had shorter front legs than back legs. This made Diplodocus one of the slowest dinosaurs. It likely only had a top speed of about 9 miles (15 km) an hour, though some scientists have estimated that it may have been able to hit speeds up to 15 miles (24 km) an hour.

Diplodocus lived in the middle part of North America. This was a lush and diverse area that included thick forests and vast savannas. It also included plenty of water sources through numerous lakes and rivers. Diplodocus shared its habitat with other sauropods, such as Apatosaurus and Brachiosaurus, as well as other well-known dinosaurs, such as Allosaurus and Stegosaurus.

Diplodocus lived about 150 million years ago during the Late Jurassic Period. It was found throughout central North America. It is here, in the present-day states of Montana, Utah, Wyoming, and Colorado, that Diplodocus fossils have been discovered. Fossils are the preserved remains of dinosaurs that died millions of years ago. The first Diplodocus fossil was discovered the new dinosaur was named the following year.

People can go to museum the Diplodocus. Diplod in the world. Several complete Hist

KEY WORDS

Research has shown that as much as 65 percent of all written material published in English is made up of 300 words. These 300 words cannot be taught using pictures or learned by sounding them out. They must be recognized by sight. This book contains 56 common sight words to help young readers improve their reading fluency and comprehension. This book also teaches young readers several important content words, such as proper nouns. These words are paired with pictures to aid in learning and improve understanding.

Page	Sight Words First Appearance	Page	Content Words First Appearance
4	her, means, name, the	4	beam, double
7	end, largest, lined, lived, longer, of, one she, than, that, to, two, up, was		Diplodocus (pronounced: dip-LOW-doe-kus)
		7	buses, dinosaurs
9	a, about, an, at, away, could, enough, make, miles, other, this, used	9	boom, hour, tail
		10	eater
10	day, every, food, many, plant	12	ground, neck
12	had, high, in, near, or, trees, very	14	legs
14	four, on, walked	15	hour, speed
16	and, rivers	16	forests, grasslands
17	part	17	North America
18	years	19	fossils
19	from, people	20	museums
20	can, go, learn, more, see